Celtic Myth Refrains
Tuatha De Danu and Welsh Cycle
Camelot Cycle

Nick Monks

Bluebell Publishing

For Amanda, Karl, Saskia

Acknowledgments- Medieval Field and Rhiannon both appeared in Dawntreader magazine. Druids was published in Dial 174.

Front cover image- Drawn by the author. Copied from Salvador Dali paintings

Poetry

By the Canal (Masque Publishing)
Winter Trees
Cities Like Jerusalem
Homes
The Love Songs of James Dyer
Narratives
Gardening
Cities Like Jerusalem (reprint edition 2)
Greek Olympian Myth
Snow
Imaginary Friends
England's of the Mind
Feminism
Explorers
American Realist Painters
Footprints (The Disparate)
The Paintings of Anslem Kiefer
The Paintings of Peter Doig
The Paintings of Gerhard Richter
The Paintings of Jean Michel Basquiat
Charlemagne's Rivers
Poems on the Paintings of Paul Klee
Poems on the Paintings of Kandinsky
Poems on the Paintings of Matisse
Snow Resume
Formby Crescent
Her Body
The Others
Ode on Darwen

Avalanche Medleys
Lovers and Tramps
The Calder's
Barry's Garage
The Jenkin's
The Blackness and Redness of Souls
The Sedge's
The Jenkin's the Early Years
Anthony and Chelsea
House Renovation and DIY
Isobel
The Moore's
A Short History of Front Doors
Robert Jenkins in 2058
Caleb Jenkins
Holly Jenkins
The Town at the End of the Peninsular
The Barnes's
Holly's Wardrobe
The Jazz Age
Pathways
Tara Worthington

Plays
Le Conquet- The Refugees

Short Stories
Aegean Islands
The Brexit British

Title Page

Published May 2021

Celtic Myth Refrains- Nick Monks

Published by Bluebell Publishing

Printed by Lulu
www.lulu.com

Celtic Myth Refrains
Nick Monks

ISBN: 978-1-008-91325-7

CONTENTS

Celtic Myth Refrains

1

Medieval Field

Two harp strings chime. Like a mermaid
Diving once more. The slopes slip into the divine;
Spaces, skeletal oaks. Frost, mist dispersing
A crescendo from the harp strings

Branwen has gone to mourn. Lugh's white stag
Bounds where Rhiannon is imprisoned as penance

As an unnamed girl lies unsettled in the shallow grave
By the swished river. Hands tied, feet bound
Hole in skull. Her ghost frantic, screaming at injustice

And with dusk. A medieval farmer, walks his land
Wood pigeon take off. He throws seeds as a gesture-
Of new life. A crow turns its head
Two more notes from harp strings.

11 Tuatha de Danu and Welsh Cycle

Branwen

Branwen has green eyes like Guinevere's
She tarry's all day on the beach
Picks up shells and beach combs the kelp tideline
Looking for periwinkles and scallop shells
Paddles bare foot in the sea
When she comes back to Conway castle

Bran the blessed and the Celtic court await her
She does not like being a princess
And wanders alone through the gorse, the heather
Misspends hours on the white sand gazing west

And one day as if foretold, the ships appeared on the horizon
The King of Ireland, Matholwch had come to betroth her
The sea waves segmented and like confetti drenched her in salt
spit.

Rhiannon
A Celtic Welsh Goddess

A lake. Shimmering silver. With no witness onlooker
Mist swirling. Revealing a divine heather moor
Were curved contours against the sky. Provide a torturous
beauty
When the snow stopped falling after 41 days and nights. Blue
snow

In the amphitheatre of lake. Sat Rhiannon on the thick ice
Her purple cape stretched. Her green eyes radiated like small
green suns

I have lived
I have loved
I have given birth
I have raised
I have worked
I have suffered
I have joyed. She says to the gods of the lake

And the high autumnal moors replied. Where now enchanted
one
She traces fingertips across the ice. The silence is deafening.
Leaf's scatter like confetti.

Meeting Lugh

For 8 days you walked north
Crossing the river Boyne and sleeping in bracken
Eating blackberry and wild garlic and hazelnut

When you found Lugh in a stone cabin
He refused to talk. And sat making iron nails and horseshoes
After 25 minutes
He raised a sword and you drew yours from the scabbard
After one ceremonial clash of swords
Lugh gave you the elixir liquid in a leather pouch

You continued to walk north. To see the Fomorians
You a lost satellite. A forward envoy. Of the Celtic battle to come
Wherein Lugh would kill Barlor. And the Tuatha De Dannan
would triumph.

Danu

Walking under beech trees. Through
Bramble thickets and deep bracken
You alight on a wood clearing

There as the light dims then is radiantly clear
A blue shimmer of light dances across

Danu becomes a beautiful Irish maid
With raven long hair. And otherworldly
Grey green eyes. You are drawn into her presence
Her eyes turn red with snake slit irises
She then becomes a shadow blue pine martin

You are in the presence of the queen of the Tuatha de Danu
Your life is changed forever
Carrying with you wings of the peregrine and
Lynx stealth. Lightning tears at the forest. New life is reborn
in you.

The soul of Celtic fire and sorrow.
Danu bequests with a glance of blue light years of light
Night passes you dream new dreams. With a Celt soul.

Mermaids 1

There are mermaids in the grey Irish sea
Due to tides and shallows and sand banks
They cannot swim into the river Douglas or Ribble

They suffer and swear and spit

They bath in star bloom light. And dive and swim
To the music of Atlantic storms and tumult of waves
When it is sunny in June they dive deep down to the sea floor -
And await the moon

At 2am you can hear there screams in Avenham park Preston
They never comb their abundant hair. In solidarity with the
human condition

They ponder mortality. And the pain of "She loves me, she loves
me not"
Mermaids can be eternal and live forever

Cold and analytical. They are constantly riven by the lure of the
human life
Their souls are uniform black
And for 4000 years they painfully ponder the rubric of: Futility.
Passion. Love and Death.

Within the kelp beds they cavort
No fisher man or ship or boat has ever seen them. Due to their
hidden furtive forever life's.

Mermaids 11

The river Lune stretches into Lancaster past Morecombe
Mermaids swim in lustrous green water
Their eyes are silver gems
They carry nothing but hope and wishes

And lounge on the silt mud banks
There songs are millennial old. And resonate
With the M6 traffic. They eat flat fish and perch
Unconcerned with human politics. They talk

To the stars the moon and waves. Eternal and beautiful
They swim in the sea and river Lune forever
And defying old lore never wish to become human
And fall in love. Enchanted they let the ebbing tide
Carry them back to the cold grey Irish sea. Whispers of
ocean waves remain and vast stretching empty sand.

Mermaids 111

Playing with dolphins and seals
Slipping stream- lined through the kelp beds

Avoiding fishermen's boats. And gas platforms
Mermaids talk to the basking sharks the shearwaters

Migrating north in April. Mermaids know each language
On earth. But talk to each other in old Arabic

They pass into the deep Atlantic past the emerald isle
They have no wish to become human. None know their
language

Or have ever seen them. Fined princesses of the salt sea and
ocean.

Druids

(While there is archaeological evidence of infrequent Celtic sacrifice.
Roman claims of wicker man sacrifice's and servants killed with their
masters are unsubstantiated)

Where the educated professional classes
Of the iron age Celts- law makers, poets, religious figures,
doctors

Glifieu and the elders and women await the return of Reghan
In the hamlet in the dark night, the bauble's of snow
flurrying

Very little is known of the Druid class
Dru-id (Oak- Knowledge) could have ceremonies
At Stonehenge temple, built around 2000BC
Druids however appear in historical records from 200BC
Next to nothing is known of their religious practices
Except the ritual of the oak and mistletoe
As described by Pliny the Elder

A teenage girl is on trial for unspecified crimes
In the Caer Bran an iron age fort in Cornwall
The river Cober swishes past
She is bound and killed with spear and club

Following the Roman invasion of Gaul
And the gradual invasion of Britain 55BC
The Druids and Celts where suppressed
By 1st C Roman emperors Claudius and Tiberius

I imagine them, the druids
In a stone circle on the Beara peninsular-
Sprinkling water on alder branches

As the families and men of the tribe watch on
And the sun is effervescently rising

Our Celt ancestors watching us in a vigil
These living ghost antecedents threading through dreams
More so for the rumour, legends, and myth
With the departure of the Romans came the Anglo Saxons
With the late 8thC came the Vikings with eyes of snow and fire.

111 Camelot Cycle

Camelot

At long tables before the castle
Dressed in white shirts and breaches
With the women in dresses
The meal of sea bass and vegetables is served

Followed by cooked seasoned apples
The chatter is a seeking for enlightenment
The group toast each other and the forested land

The group in gentle synchronicity with each other
Far away from babble noise. They consider and fall in love
again

A bonfire burns. Splinters of sparks race skyward
They dance as linnets or curlews song
And the moon rises faintly-

In a darkened sky. Camelot where apples grow year round
And the tribe await the chalice
And the sacred and divine. Like lovers do.

Antithesis of the city. An enclave of bluebell and strawberry.
Were whispers of conversation enchant by the now
Untended bonfire at 2am.

Dragon

Paces leering in front of the limestone cave
Guardian of Anwyn. Gate keeper of a new land

He breathes otherworldly fire. Red eyes like wolfs-
In Quebec car headlights. Formidable beast of warfare

The green dragon will only permit the Dragba or Danu to
enter the cave

Around are the skeletal bones and sculls of those who tried

Night now over the ancient forest
The calls of owls and mythical beasts in the forest
Star ice silver fire. Disgruntled fire breath

Within Anwyn are clear rivers, vast new lands of arcadia
And abundance.
Without is the teeming forest of beasts, wolverines, bears,
and realms. Otters shimmy in rivers of glimmering water.

And the dragon who never sleeps. Ferociously guards the
cave with razor splinter teethe and sharp iron claws.

Knights of the Round Table

Lancelot, Galahad, Percival, Mordred
And 25 other knights in attendance
The night of 3rd February 498 AD

Percival bangs his fist
The night turns to early morning
We need to send envoys north- says Galahad
They chatter
Then talk ardently of wars and of the holy chalice

Women maids were aloud to join the table
And each knight and maid spoke gallantly
Elderberry juice was drunk.
And alike Robespierre and Danton great projects
Were discussed. The large round table hosted
Many meetings. Where Camelot became

Outside of Camelot a tawny owl screeches
Softly like a divine whistle
The knights are chivalrous, valiant and brave

But after decades of fair counsel- the table breaks
And each leaves in groups. To go to war with each

And Arthur Pendragons goal is lost
As his son Mordred raises an army to the south

Tristan and Isolde

Tristan is sent to Ireland by King Mark of Cornwall
To bring back Isolde to be married

There Tristan leans over the river Liffey bridge
And walks through verdant forests

Isolde doesn't want to marry King Mark
Imperceptibly Tristan falls in love with her on sight

Then after drinking mistakenly the potion
They are matrimonially bound and inseparable
Indifferent to hardships. They elude King Mark's
Traps and snares.

Travel to Cork and Kinsale
Meet Danu. Gaze out at the green tumultuous Atlantic-
From the Beara peninsular. Entwined and in love forever.

Excalibur

Many nobles are gathered to try
And pull Excalibur from the stone
As Merlin the sage of the forest had foretold
Arthur effortlessly pulls the sword from the stone
Previously believing himself to be a serf
Non of the nobles can release the sword

In a lake of silver. Reflecting the surrounding moors
A beautiful hand appears from the centre holding
The sacred sword. Arthur takes the sword
From a small rowing boat. And is anointed king.

Merlin

Merlin walks through the alder thickets
Gazes into the silver river
When dog walkers approach he turns himself
Into a shrew. Guiding realms and kingdoms

While others live in castles or farm homesteads
Merlin walks in the forest
At ease by river or in dense trees. Always pondering
And seeking the glory of Camelot

A sage and seer and master of prophesy

He falls utterly in love with the lady of the lake
And thinks about her second by second. He dies
Leaving king Arthur pendragon on the throne on Camelot
Was buried in the sacred forest of Broceliande.

Holy Chalice

Many sought the magical keys
The sword the silver cup
That would grant access to realms and the otherworld

Only Galahad the ideal night
Picked up the silver cup. Found in a welsh turret
High on a hill.

Through wars pageant's celebrations
Long nights of discussion at the round table
It was this they sought

And the goal is near as Galahad rides
Across the heath. The knights
Once again galloping home to Camelot.

Joust

The day was fun and boisterous
Tests of strength. Horse skills. Archery.
Man to man battles with weapons

Galahad and Tristan were the last
Each had won preceding contests

They sat on fine dappled horses
And gazed across at each other
Then as moments slipped in time
And the onlooking crowd became silent

Two men in armour rode at each other
Angling the joust for the kill
Galahad struck Tristan in the chest
Tristan's joust broke. The crowd gasped
And Galahad the ideal knight had his victory

The evening after the contests
Gave way to feasts and alcohol drinks
Even showers of rain didn't hinder the joy.
The elan, the idyll. The fire at the heart of castle beauty

Soon autumn will be gone. First threa.ds of ice in the air
The ladies of the royal court. Twirl with ribbons
Around the silver birch tree trunk. The day has been good.

Guinevere

Unlike Branwen. Guinevere likes being a queen
She walks in the secret garden
In the grounds of Camelot. That only she may enter
Overgrown with blue roses and Cornish grape vines
She sits on a bench. Within the infinitesimally high walls
And ponders the royal court and the people of Briton and
France
A robin lands on her finger tip
Wherein placed is Arthurs engagement ring in silver with a
blue fluorspar gem
The elms and alder and silver birch branches stir high in the
breeze
As she ponders on the royal court
And Arthur and four knights are out in the forest hunting.

King Arthur

Awaits Guinevere arrival in the high tower room
The days battle is over
The air in the castle room is cold
Autumn is spreading ice shards on the lake
He worries of the future of the kingdom
He awaits Guinevere's arrival
The royal court is in order, he considers
The kingdom of Camelot stretches
To the serpentine rocks and gorse heath
Of the green tumultuous Atlantic
An owl calls softly from the forest
Arthur is the lord of this land of mistle thrush
Of which dark passes over the castle. He lights a candle
Awaits Guinevere. Her green eyes.

Battle of Calmann

Mordred son of Arthur awaits in the field
Once the field was for barley. The slopes slip away to trees
Now the fields here are an arena of cold war fervour
The soldiers bang iron swords on shields. No bird or mouse
answers. But a cry of defiance comes from Arthur
Pendragons men

Each wonders how they got here from farmstead hamlets
Yet they charge and wield strength to slash and thrust and
rip at the foe with iron swords.

Helmets and shields and armour are not sufficient
"So I'm dying" thinks the soldier who's guts leak from an
abdomen wound. Another man writhes with deep mortal
leg and head injuries

After the battle. Blue mist descended over the dead
Their swords where plundered
Eyes gazed in stillness. Crows alighted
The sheen of dew over breaches. Silver armour shinning

The dead talk ardently of yesteryears. Of tomorrows
Twisted bodies where they fell
Each near his neighbour. Soul mates of moveless peace
The harshness. Of battle. Now gleaming bodies on the
fragrant meadow.

And Arthur is dead. Mordred is dead. Camelot is ended

The dream is gone. Eyelids close forever. Guinevere's secret garden is sealed and the key thrown in the river Severn. The knights ride across Breton with great horse skill still. But they no longer know where they are going too. Dark the year 527 AD. Black.

Lightning Source UK Ltd.
Milton Keynes UK
UKHW021555080223
416650UK00005B/923/J